Hereward College

004159

821.92

KT-489-175

Hereward College

LEARNING RESOURCES
CENTRE

The Bees

Also by Carol Ann Duffy in Picador

The World's Wife

Feminine Gospels

Rapture

New Selected Poems

Mrs Scrooge

Love Poems

The Other Country

Another Night Before Christmas

AS EDITOR

Hand in Hand

Answering Back

To the Moon

The Bees

CAROL ANN DUFFY

PICADOR

First published 2011 by Picador
an imprint of Pan Macmillan, a division of Macmillan Publishers Limited
Pan Macmillan, 20 New Wharf Road, London N1 9RR
Basingstoke and Oxford
Associated companies throughout the world
www.panmacmillan.com

ISBN 978-0-330-44244-2

Copyright © Carol Ann Duffy 2009, 2010, 2011

Textual art © StephenRaw.com 2011

The right of Carol Ann Duffy to be identified as the
author of this work has been asserted by her in accordance
with the Copyright, Designs and Patents Act 1988.

All rights reserved. No part of this publication may be
reproduced, stored in or introduced into a retrieval system, or
transmitted, in any form, or by any means (electronic, mechanical,
photocopying, recording or otherwise) without the prior written
permission of the publisher. Any person who does any unauthorized
act in relation to this publication may be liable to criminal
prosecution and civil claims for damages.

5 7 9 8 6

A CIP catalogue record for this book is available from
the British Library.

Printed and bound by CPI Group (UK) Ltd, Croydon, CR0 4YY

Visit www.picador.com to read more about all our books
and to buy them. You will also find features, author interviews and
news of any author events, and you can sign up for e-newsletters
so that you're always first to hear about our new releases.

I Gillian Clarke,

Bardd Cenedlaethol Cymru,

Mam-gu anrhydeddus ac arbennig Ella

a'm ffrind annwyl i.

Contents

Dumb was as good as dead; better to utter

Bees are the batteries of orchards,
gardens, guard them . . .

What will you do now with the
gift of your left life?

Out of the silence, I fancied I heard the
bronze buzz of a bee . . .

The Bees

dumb was as GOOD as dead; BETTER TO UTTER

Bees

Here are my bees,
brazen, blurs on paper,
besotted; buzzwords, dancing
their flawless, airy maps.

Been deep, my poet bees,
in the parts of flowers,
in daffodil, thistle, rose, even
the golden lotus; so glide,
gilded, glad, golden, thus –

wise – and know of us:
how your scent pervades
my shadowed, busy heart,
and honey is art.

Last Post

In all my dreams, before my helpless sight,
He plunges at me, guttering, choking, drowning.

If poetry could tell it backwards, true, begin
that moment shrapnel scythed you to the stinking mud . . .
but you get up, amazed, watch bled bad blood
run upwards from the slime into its wounds;
see lines and lines of British boys rewind
back to their trenches, kiss the photographs from home –
mothers, sweethearts, sisters, younger brothers
not entering the story now
to die and die and die.
Dulce – No – Decorum – No – Pro patria mori.
You walk away.

You walk away; drop your gun (fixed bayonet)
like all your mates do too –
Harry, Tommy, Wilfred, Edward, Bert –
and light a cigarette.
There's coffee in the square,
warm French bread,
and all those thousands dead
are shaking dried mud from their hair
and queueing up for home. Freshly alive,
a lad plays Tipperary to the crowd, released
from History; the glistening, healthy horses fit for heroes, kings.

You lean against a wall,
your several million lives still possible
and crammed with love, work, children, talent, English beer, good food.
You see the poet tuck away his pocket-book and smile.

If poetry could truly tell it backwards,
then it would.

Echo

I think I was searching for treasures or stones
in the clearest of pools
when your face . . .

                  when your face,
like the moon in a well
where I might wish . . .

                        might well wish
for the iced fire of your kiss;
only on water my lips, where your face . . .

where your face was reflected, lovely,
not really there when I turned
to look behind at the emptying air . . .

the emptying air.

Scheherazade

Dumb was as good as dead;
better to utter.
Inside a bottle, a genie.
Abracadabra.
Words were a silver thread
stitching the night.
The first story I said
led to the light.

Fact was in black and white;
fiction was colour.
Inside a dragon, a jewel.
Abracadabra.
A magic carpet took flight,
bearing a girl.
The hand of a Queen shut tight
over a pearl.

Imagination was world;
clever to chatter.
Inside a she-mule, a princess.
Abracadabra.
A golden sword was hurled
into a cloud.
A dead woman unfurled
out of a shroud.

A fable spoken aloud
kindled another.
Inside a virgin, a lover.
Abracadabra.
Forty thieves in a crowd,
bearded and bold.
A lamp rubbed by a lad
turning to gold.

Talking lips don't grow cold;
babble and jabber.
Inside a beehive, a fortune.
Abracadabra.
What was lost was held
inside a tale.
The tall stories I told
utterly real.

Inside a marriage, a gaol;
better to vanish.
Inside a mirror, an ogre;
better to banish.
A thousand and one tales;
weeping and laughter.
Only the silent fail.
Abracadabra.

Big Ask

What was it Sisyphus pushed up the hill?
I wouldn't call it a rock.
Will you solemnly swear on the Bible?
I couldn't swear on a book.
With which piece did you capture the castle?
I shouldn't hazard a rook.

When did the President give you the date?
Nothing to do with Barack!
Were 1200 targets marked on a chart?
Nothing was circled in black.
On what was the prisoner stripped and stretched?
Nothing resembling a rack.

Guantanamo Bay – how many detained?
How many grains in a sack?
Extraordinary Rendition – give me some names.
How many cards in a pack?
Sexing the Dossier – name of the game?
Poker. Gin Rummy. Blackjack.

Who planned the deployment of shock and awe?
I didn't back the attack.
Inside the Mosque, please describe what you saw.
I couldn't see through the smoke.
Your estimate of the cost of the War?
I had no brief to keep track.

Where was Saddam when they found him at last?
Maybe holed under a shack.
What happened to him once they'd kicked his ass?
Maybe he swung from the neck.
The WMD . . . you found the stash?
Well, maybe not in Iraq.

Ariel

Where the bee sucks,
neonicotinoid insecticides
in a cowslip's bell lie,
in fields purple with lavender,
yellow with rape,
and on the sunflower's upturned face;
on land monotonous with cereals and grain,
merrily,
      merrily;
sour in the soil,
sheathing the seed, systemic
in the plants and crops,
the million acres to be ploughed,
seething in the orchards now,
under the blossom
             that hangs
on the bough.

Politics

How it makes your face a stone
that aches to weep, your heart a fist,
clenched or thumping, your tongue
an iron latch with no door; your right hand
a gauntlet, a glove-puppet the left, your laugh
a dry leaf twitching in the wind, your desert island discs
hiss hiss hiss, the words on your lips dice
that throw no six.
               How it takes the breath
away, the piss, your kiss a dropped pound coin,
your promises latin, feedback, static, gibberish,
your hair a wig, your gait a plankwalk. How it says
politics – to your education, fairness, health; shouts
Politics! – to your industry, investment, wealth; roars, to your
conscience, moral compass, truth, *POLITICS POLITICS*.

The Falling Soldier

after the photograph by Robert Capa

A flop back for a kip in the sun,
dropping the gun,
or a trip on a stone to send you
arse over tip
with a yelp and a curse?
No; worse. The shadow you cast
as you fall
is the start of a shallow grave.
They give medals, though,
to the grieving partners, mothers, daughters,
sons of the brave.

A breakdance to amuse your mates,
give them a laugh,
a rock'n'roll mime, Elvis time,
pretending the rifle's
just a guitar?
Worse by far. The shadow you shed
as you fall
is, brother, your soul.
They wrap you up in the flag, though,
blow a tune on a bugle before they lower you
into the hole.

A slide down a hill, your head thrown back,
daft as a boy,
and the rifle chucked away to the side
in a moment of joy,
an outburst?
Much worse. The shadow you throw
as you fall
is the shadow of death.
The camera, though,
has caught you forever and captured forever
your final breath.

Mrs Schofield's GCSE

You must prepare your bosom for his knife,
said Portia to Antonio in which
of Shakespeare's Comedies? Who killed his wife,
insane with jealousy? And which Scots witch
knew *Something wicked this way comes*? Who said
Is this a dagger which I see? Which Tragedy?
Whose blade was drawn which led to Tybalt's death?
To whom did dying Caesar say *Et tu*? And why?
Something is rotten in the state of Denmark – do you
know what this means? Explain how poetry
pursues the human like the smitten moon
above the weeping, laughing earth; how we
make prayers of it. *Nothing will come of nothing:*
speak again. Said by which King? You may begin.

Poetry

I couldn't see Guinness
and not envisage a nun;
a gun, a finger and thumb;
midges, blether, scribble, scrum.

A crescent moon, boomerang, smirk,
bone; or full, a shield, a stalker,
a stone. I couldn't see woods
for the names of trees – sycamore,
yew, birch, beech –

        or bees
without imagining music scored
on the air – nor pass a nun
without calling to mind a pint of one, stout,
untouched, on a bar at the Angelus.

Achilles

Myth's river – where his mother dipped him,
fished him, a slippery golden boy –
flowed on, his name on its lips.
Without him, it was prophesied,
they would not take Troy.

Women hid him, concealed him in girls' sarongs;
days of sweetmeats, spices, silver song . . .
but when Odysseus came,
with an athlete's build, a sword and a shield,
he followed him to the battlefield,
the crowd's roar,
               and it was sport, not war,
his charmed foot on the ball . . .

but then his heel, his heel, his heel . . .

The Shirt

Afterwards, I found him alone at the bar
and asked him what went wrong. *It's the shirt,*
he said. *When I pull it on it hangs on my back*
like a shroud, or a poisoned jerkin from Grimm
seeping its curse onto my skin, the worst tattoo.
I shower and shave before I shrug on the shirt,
smell like a dream; but the shirt sours my scent
with the sweat and stink of fear. It's got my number.
I poured him another shot. *Speak on, my son.* He did.
I've wanted to sport the shirt since I was a kid,
but now when I do it makes me sick, weak, paranoid.
All night above the team hotel, the moon is the ball
in a penalty kick. Tens of thousands of fierce stars
are booing me. A screech owl is the referee.
The wind's a crowd, forty years long, bawling a filthy song
about my Wag. It's the bloody shirt! He started to blub
like a big girl's blouse and I felt a fleeting pity.
Don't cry, I said, *at the end of the day you'll be stiff*
in a shirt of solid gold, shining for City.

Oxfam

A silvery, pale-blue satin tie, freshwater in sunlight, 50p.
Charlotte Rhead, hand-painted oval bowl, circa 1930, perfect
for apples, pears, oranges a child's hand takes without
a second thought, £80. Rows of boots marking time, £4.
Shoes like history lessons, £1.99. That jug, 30p, to fill with milk.
That mirror, £5, to look yourself in the eye. A commemoration
plate, 23 July 1986, marriage of HRH Prince Andrew
to Miss Sarah Ferguson, £2.99, size of a landmine.
Rare 1st ed. Harry Potter and the Philosopher's Stone, signed
by the author – like magic, a new school – £9000. Pen, 10p.
Pair of spectacles (longsight) £3. P/b Fieldnotes from a Catastrophe:
Report on Climate Change by Elizabeth Kolbert (hindsight) 40p.
Jade earrings and necklace, somewhere a mother, £20, brand new
gentleman's suit, somewhere a brother, £30. All Fairtrade.

The Female Husband

Having been, in my youth, a pirate
with cutlass and parrot, a gobful of bad words
yelled at the salty air to curse a cur to the end
of a plank; having jumped ship

                            in a moonstruck port,
opened an evil bar – a silver coin for a full flask,
a gold coin for don't ask – and boozed and bragged
with losers and hags for a year; having disappeared,

a new lingo's herby zest on my tongue,
to head South on a mule, where a bandit man
took *gringo* me to the heart of his gang; having robbed
the bank, the coach, the train, the saloon, outdrawn

the sheriff, the deputy sheriff, the deputy's deputy, caught
the knife of an enemy chief in my teeth; having crept away
from the camp fire, clipped upstream for a night
and a day on a stolen horse,

                        till I reached the tip
of the century and the lip of the next – it was nix to me
to start again with a new name, a stranger to fame.
Which was how I came to this small farm,

                              the love of my life
on my arm, tattooed on my wrist,
where we have cows and sheep and hens and geese
and keep good bees.

BEES
are the
batteries
of
ORChards,
gardens,
Guard
them...

Virgil's Bees

Bless air's gift of sweetness, honey
from the bees, inspired by clover,
marigold, eucalyptus, thyme,
the hundred perfumes of the wind.
Bless the beekeeper

              who chooses for her hives
a site near water, violet beds, no yew,
no echo. Let the light lilt, leak, green
or gold, pigment for queens,
and joy be inexplicable but *there*
in harmony of willowherb and stream,
of summer heat and breeze,
                    each bee's body
at its brilliant flower, lover-stunned,
strumming on fragrance, smitten.

                  For this,
let gardens grow, where beelines end,
sighing in roses, saffron blooms, buddleia;
where bees pray on their knees, sing, praise
in pear trees, plum trees; bees
are the batteries of orchards, gardens, guard them.

Rings

I might have raised your hand to the sky
to give you the ring surrounding the moon
or looked to twin the rings of your eyes
with mine
        or added a ring to the rings of a tree
by forming a handheld circle with you, thee,
or walked with you
            where a ring of church-bells
looped the fields,
or kissed a lipstick ring on your cheek,
a pressed flower,
        or met with you
in the ring of an hour,
and another hour . . .
        I might
have opened your palm to the weather, turned, turned,
till your fingers were ringed in rain
or held you close,
        they were playing our song,
in the ring of a slow dance
or carved our names
in the rough ring of a heart
or heard the ring of an owl's hoot
as we headed home in the dark
or the ring, first thing,
        of chorusing birds
waking the house
or given the ring of a boat, rowing the lake,
or the ring of swans, monogamous, two,

or the watery rings made by the fish
as they leaped and splashed
or the ring of the sun's reflection there . . .
I might have tied
                  a blade of grass,
a green ring for your finger,
or told you the ring of a sonnet by heart
or brought you a lichen ring,
found on a warm wall,
or given a ring of ice in winter
                          or in the snow
sung with you the five gold rings of a carol
or stolen a ring of your hair
or whispered the word in your ear
that brought us here,
where nothing and no one is wrong,
and therefore I give you this ring.

Invisible Ink

When Anon, no one now,
knew for sure the *cu* and *koo*
he spelled from his mouth
could put the tribe in sight
of a call they'd met before
in their ears, the air ever after was
invisible ink.

       Then, *hey nonny no*,
the poets came; rhyme, metre,
metaphor, there for the taking
for every chancer or upstart crow
in hedgerow, meadow, forest, pool;
shared words, vast same poem
for all to write.

       I snap a twig
from a branch as I walk, sense
the nib of it dip and sip, dip
and sip, a first draft of the gift –
anonymous yet – texted from heart
to lips; my hand dropping a wand
into this fluent, glittery stream.

Atlas

Give him strength, crouched on one knee in the dark
with the Earth on his back,
                         balancing the seven seas,
the oceans, five, kneeling
in ruthless, empty, endless space
                         for grace
of whale, dolphin, sea-lion, shark, seal, fish, every kind
which swarms the waters. Hero.

                         Hard, too,
heavy to hold, the mountains;
burn of his neck and arms taking the strain –
Andes, Himalayas, Kilimanjaro –
give him strength, he heaves them high
to harvest rain from skies for streams
and rivers, he holds the rivers,
holds the Amazon, Ganges, Nile, hero, hero.

Hired by no one, heard in a myth only, lonely,
he carries a planet's weight,
                         islands and continents,
the billions there, his ears the last to hear
their language, music, gunfire, prayer;
give him strength, strong girth, for elephants,
tigers, snow leopards, polar bears, bees, bats,
the last ounce of a hummingbird.

                              Broad-backed
in infinite, bleak black,
                    he bears where Earth is, nowhere,
head bowed, a genuflection to the shouldered dead,
the unborn's hero, he is love's lift;
sometimes the moon rolled to his feet, given.

John Barleycorn

Although I knew they'd laid him low,
thrashed him, hung him out to dry,
had tortured him with water and with fire,
then dashed his brains out on a stone,
I saw him in the Seven Stars
and in the Plough.
I saw him in the Crescent Moon
and in the Beehive and the Barley Mow,
my green man, newly-born, alive, John Barleycorn.

I saw him seasonally, at harvest time
in the Wheatsheaf and the Load of Hay.
I saw him, heard his laughter,
in the Star and Garter, in the Fountain, in the Bell,
the Corn Dolly, the Woolpack and the Flowing Spring.
I saw him in the Rising Sun,
the Moon and Sixpence and the Evening Star.
I saw him in the Rose and Crown,
my green man, ancient, barely born, John Barleycorn.

He moved through Britain, bright and dark
like ale in glass. I saw him run across the fields
towards the Gamekeeper, the Poacher and the Blacksmith's Arms.
He knew the Ram, the Lamb, the Lion and the Swan,
White Hart, Blue Boar, Red Dragon, Fox and Hounds.
I saw him in the Three Goats' Heads,
the Black Bull and Dun Cow,
Shoulder of Mutton, Griffin, Unicorn,
green man, beer borne, good health, long life, John Barleycorn.

I saw him festively, when people sang
for victory, or love, or New Year's Eve,
in the Raven and the Bird in Hand,
the Golden Eagle, the Kingfisher, the Dove.
I saw him grieve, or mourn, a shadow at the bar
in the Falcon, the Marsh Harrier, the Sparrow Hawk,
the Barn Owl, Cuckoo, Heron, Nightingale;
a pint of bitter in the Jenny Wren
for my green man, alone, forlorn, John Barleycorn.

Britain's soul, as the crow flies so flew he.
I saw him in the Hollybush, the Yew Tree,
the Royal Oak, the Ivy Bush, the Linden.
I saw him in the Forester, the Woodman.
He history, I saw him in the Wellington, the Nelson,
Greyfriars Bobby, Wicked Lady, Bishop's Finger.
I saw him in the Ship, the Golden Fleece, the Flask,
the Railway Inn, the Robin Hood and Little John,
my green man, legend strong, re-born, John Barleycorn.

Scythed down, he crawled, knelt, stood.
I saw him in the Crow, Newt, Stag, all weathers,
noon or night. I saw him in the Feathers, Salutation,
Navigation, Knot, the Bricklayer's Arms, Hop Inn,
the Maypole and the Regiment, the Horse and Groom,
the Dog and Duck, the Flag. And where he supped,
the past lived still; and where he sipped, the glass brimmed full.
He was in the King's Head and Queen's Arms, I saw him there,
green man, well-born, spellbound, charming one, John Barleycorn.

Hive

All day we leave and arrive at the hive,
concelebrants. The hive is love,
what we serve, preserve, avowed in Latin murmurs
as we come and go, skydive, freighted
with light, to where we thrive, us, in time's hum,
on history's breath,

                            industrious, identical . . .

there suck we,
alchemical, nectar-slurred, pollen-furred,
the world's mantra us, our blurry sound
along the thousand scented miles to the hive,
haven, where we unpack our foragers;
or heaven-stare, drone-eyed, for a queen's star;
or nurse or build in milky, waxy caves,
the hive, alive, us – how we behave.

Nile

When I went, wet, wide, white and blue, my name Nile,
you'd kneel near to net fish, or would wade
where I shallowed, or swim in my element,
or sing a lament for the child drowned where I was too deep,
too fast; but once you found, in my reeds,
a boy in a basket.
                    I gushed, fresh lake, salt sea,
utterly me, source to mouth, without me, drought, nought,
for my silt civilized –
                    from my silt, pyramids.
Where I went, undammed, talented,
food, wine, work, craft, art;
no Nile, nil, null, void.
                    I poured, full spate, roared,
voiced water, calling you in from dust, thirst, burn,
to where you flourished; Pharaoh, firstborn . . .
now Cleopatra's faint taste still on my old tongue.

Water

Your last word was *water*,
which I poured in a hospice plastic cup, held
to your lips – your small sip, half-smile, sigh –
then, in the chair beside you,
                                    fell asleep.

Fell asleep for three lost hours,
only to waken, thirsty, hear then see
a magpie warn in a bush outside –
dawn so soon – and swallow from your still-full cup.

Water. The times I'd call as a child
for a drink, till you'd come, sit on the edge
of the bed in the dark, holding my hand,
just as we held hands now and you died.

A good last word.
                          Nights since I've cried, but gone
to my own child's side with a drink, watched
her gulp it down then sleep. *Water.*
What a mother brings
                              through darkness still
to her parched daughter.

Drams

The snows melt early,
meeting river and valley,
greeting the barley.

*

In Glen Strathfarrar
a stag dips to the river
where rainclouds gather.

*

Dawn, offered again,
and heather sweetens the air.
I sip at nothing.

*

A cut-glass tumbler,
himself splashing the amber . . .
now I remember.

*

Beautiful hollow
by the broad bay; safe haven;
their Gaelic namings.

*

It was Talisker
on your lips, peppery, sweet,
I tasted, kisser.

*

Under the table
she drank him, my grandmother,
Irish to his Scotch.

*

Barley, water, peat,
weather, landscape, history;
malted, swallowed neat.

*

Out on Orkney's boats,
spicy, heather-honey notes
into our glad throats.

*

Allt Dour Burn's water –
pure as delight, light's lover –
burn of the otter.

*

The gifts to noses –
bog myrtle, aniseed, hay,
attar of roses.

*

Empty sherry casks,
whisky – *sublime accident* –
a Spanish accent.

*

Drams with a brother
and doubles with another . . .
blether then bother.

*

The perfume of place,
seaweed scent on peaty air,
heather dabbed with rain.

*

With Imlah, Lochhead,
Dunn, Jamie, Paterson, Kay,
Morgan, with MacCaig.

*

Not prose, poetry;
crescendo of mouth music;
not white wine, whisky.

*

*Eight bolls of malt, to
Friar John Cor, wherewith to
make aquavitae.*

*

A recurring dream:
men in hats taking a dram
on her coffin lid.

*

The sad flit from here
to English soil, English air,
from whisky to beer.

*

For joy, grief, trauma,
for the newly-wed, the dead –
bitter-sweet water.

*

A quaich; Highland Park;
our shared sips in the gloaming
by the breathing loch.

*

The unfinished dram
on the hospice side-table
as the sun came up.

*

What the heron saw,
the homesick salmon's shadow,
shy in this whisky.

Moniack Mhor

Something is dealing from a deck of cards,
face up, seven, a week of mornings, today's
revealing the hills at Moniack Mhor, shrugging off
their mists. A sheepdog barks six fields away;
I see the farm from here.

Twelve-month cards, each one thumbed, flipped,
weathered in its way – this the eighth, harvest-time,
a full moon like a trump, a magic trick.
It rose last night above this house, affirmative.
I sensed your answer – hearts.

Or a single hour is a smiling Jack, a diamond,
or a spade learning a grave; charms or dark lessons.
Something is shuffling; the soft breath of Moniack Mhor
on the edge of utterance, I know it, the verbs of swifts
riffling the air

and the road turning itself into the loch, a huge ace
into which everything folds. Here is the evening,
displayed then dropped to drift to the blazon of barley, bracken,
heather. Something is gifting this great gold gathering of cloud;
a continual farewell.

The English Elms

Seven Sisters in Tottenham,
long gone, except for their names,
were English elms.

Others stood at the edge of farms,
twinned with the shapes of clouds
like green rhymes;
or cupped the beads of rain
in their leaf palms;
or glowered, grim giants, warning of storms.

In the hedgerows in old films,
elegiacally, they loom,
the English elms;
or find posthumous fame
in the lines of poems –
the music making elm –
for ours is a world without them . . .

to whom the artists came,
time upon time,
scumbling, paint on their fingers and thumbs;
and the woodcutters, who knew the elm
was a coffin's deadly aim;
and the mavis, her filled nest unharmed
in the crook of a living, wooden arm;
and boys, with ball, bat, stumps
for a game;
and nursing ewes and lambs, calm
under English elms . . .

great, masterpiece trees
who were overwhelmed.

The Counties

But I want to write to an Essex girl,
greeting her warmly.
But I want to write to a Shropshire lad,
brave boy, home from the Army,
and I want to write to the Lincolnshire Poacher
to hear of his hare
and to an aunt in Bedfordshire
who makes a wooden hill of her stair.
But I want to post a rose to a Lancashire lass,
red, I'll pick it,
and I want to write to a Middlesex mate
for tickets for cricket.
But I want to write to the Ayrshire cheesemaker
and his good cow
and it is my duty to write to The Queen at Berkshire
in praise of Slough.
But I want to write to the National Poet of Wales at Ceredigion
in celebration
and I want to write to the Dorset Giant
in admiration
and I want to write to a widow in Rutland
in commiseration
and to the Inland Revenue in Yorkshire
in desperation.
But I want to write to my uncle in Clackmannanshire
in his kilt
and to my scrumptious cousin in Somerset
with her cidery lilt.

But I want to write to two ladies in Denbighshire,
near Llangollen
and I want to write to a laddie in Lanarkshire,
Dear Lachlan . . .
But I want to write to the Cheshire Cat,
returning its smile.
But I want to write the names of the Counties down
for my own child
and may they never be lost to her . . .
all the birds of Oxfordshire and Gloucestershire . . .

The White Horses

The earth's heart hears hooves
under hillsides,
                thunder in Wiltshire;
and the glistening rain, in wet hours,
all ears for the white horses, listens;
the wind, hoarse, gargles
breath and whinny and shriek.
The moon's chalk face pines for her foals.

But the sky swears
                the white horses
are dropped clouds;
the sea vows they came from a wave,
foamy, salt-maned, galloping inland;
death claims it will set them
to pulling a hearse,
                and love
goes riding, all night, bareback,
hunting itself.

They dreamed them, the local dead,
ghosts of war-horses,
                              warriors', heroes',
asleep in the landscape;
woke to the white horses shining
high over woods and farms;
young ancestors working the fields,
naming them his, hers, ours.
They sensed them, pulling the county
deep into England,
harnessed, history's;
                              their scent sweet on the air –
wheat, hops, hay, chalk, clay.
Then stars nailed shoes to their hooves.

The conservationists climb the hills
away from their cars,
                              new leucippotomists
with implements to scour and groom,
scrub and comb.
                      On a clear day,
from twenty miles,
                              a driver sees a white horse
printing its fresh, old form on turf
like a poem.

Luke Howard, Namer of Clouds

Eldezar and Asama Yama, 1783,
erupted violently; a *Great Fogg*
blending incredible skies over Europe.
In London, Luke Howard was ten.
The sky's lad then.

                    Smitten,
he stared up evermore; saw
a meteor's fiery spurt,
the clamouring stars;
what the moon wouldn't do;
but loved clouds most –
dragons and unicorns;
Hamlet's camels, weasels and whales;
the heads of heroes;
the sword of Excalibur, lit
by the setting sun.
                    Mackerel sky,
mackerel sky, not long wet,
not long dry.

                    And knew
love goes naming,
even a curl of hair – thus, Cirrus.
Cumulus. Stratus. Nimbus.

What WILL YOU DO NOW WITH THE GIFT of YOUR REST of LIFE?

The Woman in the Moon

Darlings, I write to you from the moon
where I hide behind famous light.
How could you think it ever a man up here?
A cow jumped over. The dish ran away with

the spoon. What reached me were your joys, griefs,
here's-the-craic, losses, longings, your lives
brief, mine long, a talented loneliness. I must have
a thousand names for the earth, my blue vocation.

Round I go, the moon a diet of light, sliver of pear,
wedge of lemon, slice of melon, half an orange,
silver onion; your human sound falling through space,
childbirth's song, the lover's song, the song of death.

Devoted as words to things, I gaze, gawp, glare; deserts
where forests were, sick seas. When night comes,
I see you gaping back as though you hear my *Darlings,
what have you done, what have you done to the world?*

Parliament

Then in the writers' wood,
every bird with a name in the world
crowded the leafless trees,
took its turn to whistle or croak.
An owl grieved in an oak.
A magpie mocked. A rook
cursed from a sycamore.
The cormorant spoke:
                                    Stinking seas
below ill winds. Nothing swims.
A vast plastic soup, thousand miles
wide as long, of petroleum crap.

A bird of paradise wept in a willow.
The jewel of a hummingbird shrilled
on the air.
A stork shawled itself like a widow.
The gull said:
Where coral was red, now white, dead
under stunned waters.
The language of fish
cut out at the root.
Mute oceans. Oil like a gag
on the Gulf of Mexico.

A woodpecker heckled.
A vulture picked at its own breast.
Thrice from the cockerel, as ever.
The macaw squawked:
>   *Nouns I know –*
Rain. Forest. Fire. Ash.
Chainsaw. Cattle. Cocaine. Cash.
Squatters. Ranchers. Loggers. Looters.
Barons. Shooters.

A hawk swore.
A nightingale opened its throat
in a garbled quote.
A worm turned in the blackbird's beak.
This from the crane:
What I saw – slow thaw
in permafrost; broken terrain
of mud and lakes;
peat broth; seepage; melt;
methane breath.

A bat hung like a suicide.
Only a rasp of wings from the raven.
A heron was stone; a robin blood
in the written wood.
So snow and darkness slowly fell;
the eagle, history, in silhouette,
with the golden plover,
and the albatross
>   telling of Arctic ice
as the cold, hard moon calved from the earth.

Telling the Bees

When I went to read
the bulletin about broken holy beads
to the bees,
the beads were the bees themselves . . .

(though once I'd been
a bairn with a bamboo-cane,
keen to follow the beekeeper
down to the hives, tap and tell
all news – whose bride, who lied, who'd died –
and had seen the bees as a rosary, girdling,
garden by garden, the land;
or had heard their hard devotional sound
in the ears of flowers
as I barely breathed, beheld
their bold, intimate touch . . .)

for a scattered bracelet of bees
lay on the grass by their burgled hive.

So how could I tell the bees?

Black blood in the sea.
Corn buttercup brought to its knee.
No honey for tea.

Dorothy Wordsworth is Dead

who came to lose every tooth in her head;
fierce maid, who saw the crowfoot
as a spinster friend; found, in the russet fronds
of Osmunda ferns, fervour;

                            feared cows;
on all fours crawled
home through a thunderstorm;
walked five miles each way, each day,
in hope of letters; thin scrap, work-worn,
her black frock mud-hemmed;

                      Dorothy,
green gold of moss in her loose purse, gatherer,
who thought strawberry blossom *brave*
in its early grave of rock; had quick birds
for her own eyes from watching them:
the robin's blushing bounce,
the magpie's funeral chic,
the heron's grief,
               grief . . .

whose tongue travelled her empty gums
on her long lake treks;
                          but was loved yet,
sharp lass, noticer; all ears, years,
for the wind's thumb on the latch;
first to spy – *o sister* –
the moon's eye at the glass,
two stars squinting . . .

                          and cold in her bed
uttered flowers, *hepatica, daffodil, anemone,*
crocus,
          as a corpse in its manner does
in St. Oswald's churchyard under the yews
her brother planted;
and trudged or lay by him till he kindled.

Cockermouth and Workington

No folk fled the flood,
no flags furled or spirits failed –
one brave soul felled.

Fouled fortune followed,
but families filed into the fold
for a fire flared.

They were floored,
a few said fooled; no – fuelled
by fellow-feeling, hearts full.

New bridge now, small fords;
farmhands in foaled fields.

Spell

Yes, I think a poem is a spell of kinds
that keeps things living in a written line,
whatever's lost or leaving – lock of rhyme –
and so I write and write and write your name.

Simon Powell

What was your appeal, Simon Powell?
Your silver smile;
how you held your face aloft,
a trophy, when you laughed.
You had style,
swooping towards Swansea
on your Moto Morini,
brave, *bravo!*, pale rider.

Whom did you beguile, Simon Powell,
on that ferry in Liverpool?
A poetry girl. Well, well,
you were always poetry's proud pal;
she was bound to chime with you
eventually,
             vowel to pure vowel –
poetry and Simon Powell.

Our days continue to delight us, or appal,
like yours: the birth of sons,
the death of Siân;
then to your Indian wedding on a horse,
your thousand nights; blessed, you told us,
Simon Powell, in your wives,
the seeded futures of your three boys' lives;
as we by thee, dear Simon; Simon Powell.

Cold

It felt so cold, the snowball which wept in my hands,
and when I rolled it along in the snow, it grew
till I could sit on it, looking back at the house,
where it was cold when I woke in my room, the windows
blind with ice, my breath undressing itself on the air.
Cold, too, embracing the torso of snow which I lifted up
in my arms to build a snowman, my toes, burning, cold
in my winter boots; my mother's voice calling me in
from the cold. And her hands were cold from peeling
and pooling potatoes into a bowl, stooping to cup
her daughter's face, a kiss for both cold cheeks, my cold nose.
But nothing so cold as the February night I opened the door
in the Chapel of Rest where my mother lay, neither young, nor old,
where my lips, returning her kiss to her brow, knew the meaning of cold.

The Bee Carol

Silently on Christmas Eve,
the turn of midnight's key;
all the garden locked in ice –
a silver frieze –
except the winter cluster of the bees.

Flightless now and shivering,
around their Queen they cling;
every bee a gift of heat;
she will not freeze
within the winter cluster of the bees.

Bring me for my Christmas gift
a single golden jar;
let me taste the sweetness there,
but honey leave
to feed the winter cluster of the bees.

Come with me on Christmas Eve
to see the silent hive –
trembling stars cloistered above –
and then believe,
bless the winter cluster of the bees.

Decembers

The single bed
was first a wooden boat;
stars translated for me
as I drifted away –
our cargoed winter house
dark and at anchor –

and then a Russian Doll
where I stilled in my selves;
six secrets or presents
under a thrilled tree.

I saw a coffin, shouldered
through snow, shrouded
in its cold, laced sheet.
Now, delirious bells
shaking this small spare room
on Christmas morning.

Winter's Tale

Tell she is well in these arms;
synonymous, her heartbeat to mine;
the world a little room; undone
all hurt; her inbreath, breath,
love where death, where harm, hope,
flesh where stone; my line – *O*
she's warm! – charm, blessing, prayer,
spell; outwith dream, without time;
enchantment tell, garden from grave
to garland her; above these worms,
violet, oxlip, primrose, columbine;
she wakes, moves, prompted by her name.

Snow

Then all the dead opened their cold palms
and released the snow; slow, slant, silent,
a huge unsaying, it fell, torn language, settled;
the world to be locked, local; unseen,
fervent earthbound bees around a queen.
The river grimaced and was ice.

                              Go nowhere –
thought the dead, using the snow –
but where you are, offering the flower of your breath
to the white garden, or seeds to birds
from your living hand. You cannot leave.
Tighter and tighter, the beautiful snow
holds the land in its fierce embrace.
It is like death, but it is not death; lovelier.
Cold, inconvenienced, late, what will you do now
with the gift of your left life?

Crunch

It's snowing! Twelve, she runs outside into the cold.
I follow from the kitchen, in my hand an apple
I was about to peel and core. She squeals, loud,
snowflakes melting on her tongue, then topples
down, cartoon joyful, brightly young. Here come the dogs,
hilariously perplexed, barking at the ghosts of plants,
biting the sky. Last weekend, burglars came – *Be drugs,*
the policeman said, *or credit crunch* – taking their chance,
the Visa, chequebook, presents underneath the tree,
laptop, TV. I watch snow deepen, settle hard,
like . . . which simile? Like debt? Like poverty? . . .
imagine some gloved hand insert my useless cards
into the wall, that other life; then *What's for lunch?*
she bawls. I throw the apple, happy, hear the crunch.

A Goldfish

I bought, on a whim, a goldfish for a good girl.
It swam in an antique bowl in the kitchen there,
creative among the lentils and the marmalade,
painting itself over and over, self-portrait in liquid;
learning its letter, O for oxygen, for only.

                                    It seemed fulfilled;
the halo of its constant swim unrolling a pond
below willow trees, an imperial palace garden
where the poet sat, floating on silence; a mouth opening
to gold: walking towards her, carrying fragrant tea,
her beloved, favourite child.

OUT OF THE
SILENCE,
I FANCIED I
HEARD THE
BRONZE
BUZZ
OF A BEE...

Music

Do you think they cried, the children
who followed the Piper, when the rock
closed behind them forever; or cried never,
happy to dance to his tune, lost
in the music?
                              And the lame boy,
pressing his ear to locked stone
to carry an echo home in his head,
did he weep, alone, the melody gone? Tell me

who hasn't tossed a coin in a hat
for the busker on blues harmonica, heartbreak
in the rain;
                              or stood in the square
by the students there, cheap violins
gleaming under their chins, the Bach Double
clapped by pigeons;
                                        or smiled at the ragged choir
rattling their tins? What's music
the food of? Send over a beer
to the bow-tied piano man to play it again . . .

a child's hands
on the keys, opening a scale
like a toy of sound . . .

and who hasn't lifted the lid
to pick at a tune with a fingertip –
Perfect Day, Danny Boy, Für Elise –
recalling a name, or a kiss;
the breath our lips shared,
unsung song?

        When the light's gone,
it's what the dying choose,
the music we use at funerals –
psalms listed in roman numerals;
solo soprano singing to a grave;
sometimes the pipes, a harp.
Do you think music hath charms?
Do you think it hears and heals our hearts?

Orta St Giulio

My beautiful daughter stands by the lake
at Orta St Giulio; the evening arriving, dressed
in its milky, turquoise silks, her fortune foretold;
assonant mountains and clouds all around;
an aptness of bells from here, there, there, there. *Ella.*

I watch her film the little fish
which flop, slap, leap in the water, hear
her hiss *yes, yes,* as she zooms on fresh verbs
and my heart makes its own small flip.
I slip behind her into the future; memory.

A bat swoops, the lake a silence of dark light;
how it will be, must be.

The Dead

They're very close to us, the dead;
us in our taxis, them in their hearses,
waiting for the lights to change.
We give them precedence.

So close to us, unknown on television;
dead from hunger, earthquake, war,
suicide bomber, tsunami.
We count the numbers.

The famous dead – a double glamour –
we buy their music, movies, memoirs.
O! Elizabeth Taylor as Cleopatra
in glorious technicolor.

In Venice, we glimpse the dead
drift to the island cemetery across the lagoon.
We float our gondolas along the green canals
and do not die.

Sung

Now only words in a song,
no more than a name
on a stone,
and that well overgrown –
MAR– –ORIS– –;

and wind though a ruined croft,
the door an appalled mouth,
the window's eye put out;

hours and wishes and trysts
less than shadows of bees on grass,
ghosts that did dance, did kiss . . .

those who would gladly die for love long dead –
a skull for a bonnie head –
and love a simile, a rose, red, red.

At Ballynahinch

I lay on the bank at Ballynahinch
and saw the light hurl down
like hammers flung by the sun
to light-stun me, batter
the water to pewter,
everything dream or myth,
my own death further upstream;
the sleeping breath now – by my side
in our wounded sprawl – of the one
who did not love me at all,
who had never loved me, no,
who would never love me, I knew,
down by the star-thrashed river at Ballynahinch,
at Ballynahinch, at Ballynahinch.

New Vows

From this day forth to unhold,
to see the nothing in ringed gold,
uncare for you when you are old.

New vows you make me swear to keep –
not ever wake with you, or sleep,
or your body, with mine, worship;

this empty hand slipped from your glove,
these lips sip never from our loving cup,
I may not cherish, kiss; unhave, unlove . . .

And all my worldly goods to unendow . . .
And who here present upon whom I call . . .

Leda

Obsessed by faithfulness,
                    I went to the river
where the swans swam in their pairs and saw how a heart
formed in the air as they touched, partnered forever.
Under the weeping trees a lone swan swam apart.

I knelt like a bride as bees hymned in the clover
and he rose, huge, an angel, out of the water,
to cover me, my billed, feathered, webbed, winged lover;
a chaos of passion beating the fair day whiter.

My hands, frantic to hold him, felt flight, force, friction,
his weird beautiful form rising and falling above –
the waxy, intimate creak –
                    as though he might fly,
turn all my unborn children into fiction.
I knew their names that instant, pierced by love
and by the song the swans sing as they die.

Valentine's

Pain past bearing, poetry's price,
to know which of the harms and hurts
dealt to you, to the day, was fatal;
a kick to the heart by the ghost of a mule
you thought to ride to your wedding-feast.

But now you can snip that shadow
from your heels for mourning-dress
or go to hell in a handcart, along
with the rest of our helpless world;
and, O, if you could, you would,
where lovers walked, sell off the trees
and not give a flying fuck for
the muted mausoleums of the bees.

The Human Bee

I became a human bee at twelve,
when they gave me my small wand,
my flask of pollen,
and I walked with the other bees
out to the orchards.

I worked first in apples,
                              climbed the ladder
into the childless arms of a tree
and busied myself, dipping and tickling,
duping and tackling, tracing
the petal's guidelines
down to the stigma.
                              Human, humming,
I knew my lessons by heart:
the ovary would become the fruit,
the ovule the seed,
fertilized by my golden touch,
my Midas dust.

I moved to lemons,
                              head and shoulders
lost in blossom; dawn till dusk,
my delicate blessing.
All must be docile, kind, unfraught
for one fruit –
                              pomegranate, lychee,
nectarine, peach, the rhymeless orange.
And if an opening bud
                              was out of range,
I'd jump from my ladder onto a branch
and reach.

So that was my working life as a bee,
till my eyesight blurred,
my hand was a trembling bird
                              in the leaves,
the bones of my fingers thinner than wands.
And when they retired me,
I had my wine from the silent vines,
and I'd known love,
and I'd saved some money –

but I could not fly and I made no honey.

Drone

An upward rush on stairs of air
to the bliss of nowhere, higher,
a living jewel, warm amber, her,
to be the one who would die there.

Gesture

Did you know your hands could catch that dark hour
like a ball, throw it away into long grass
and when you looked again at your palm, there
was your life-line, shining?
                              Or when death came,
with its vicious, biting bark, at a babe,
your whole body was brave;
or came with its boiling burns,
your arms reached out, love's gesture.
                              Did you know
when cancer draped its shroud on your back,
you'd make it a flag;
or ignorance smashed its stones through glass,
light, you'd see, in shards;
paralysed, walk; traumatised, talk?
                              Did you know
at the edge of your ordinary, human days
the gold of legend blazed,
where you kneeled by a wounded man,
or healed a woman?
                    Know –
your hand is a star.
Your blood is famous in your heart.

Passing-Bells

That moment when the soldier's soul
slipped through his wounds, seeped
through the staunching fingers of his friend
then, like a shadow, slid across a field
to vanish, vanish, into textless air . . .
there would have been a bell in Perth,
Llandudno, Bradford, Winchester,
rung by a landlord in a sweating, singing pub
or by an altar-boy at Mass – in Stoke-on-Trent,
Leicester, Plymouth, Crewe, in Leeds, Stockport,
Littleworth – an ice-cream van jingling in a park;
a door pushed open to a jeweller's shop;
a songbird fluttering from a tinkling cat – in Ludlow,
Wolverhampton, Taunton, Hull – a parish church
chiming out the hour; the ringing end of school –
in Wigan, Caythorpe, Peterborough, Ipswich,
Aberdeen, King's Lynn, Malvern, Poole –
a deskbell in a quiet, dark hotel; bellringers' practice
heard by Sunday cricketers; the first of midnight's bells
at Hogmanay –in Huddersfield, Motherwell, Rhyl –
there would have been a bell in Chester,
Fife, Bridgend, Wells, Birkenhead, Newcastle,
in city and in town and countryside –
the crowded late night bus; a child's bicycle;
the old, familiar, clanking cow-bells of the cattle.

Premonitions

We first met when your last breath
cooled in my palm like an egg;
you dead, and a thrush outside
sang it was morning.
I backed out of the room, feeling
the flowers freshen and shine in my arms.

The night before, we met again, to unsay
unbearable farewells, to see
our eyes brighten with re-strung tears.
O I had my sudden wish –
though I barely knew you –
to stand at the door of your house,
feeling my heartbeat calm,
as they carried you in, home, home and healing.
Then slow weeks, removing the wheelchair, the drugs,
the oxygen mask and tank, the commode,
the appointment cards,
until it was summer again
and I saw you open the doors to the grace of your garden.

Strange and beautiful to see
the flowers close to their own premonitions,
the grass sweeten and cool and green
where a bee swooned backwards out of a rose.
There you were,
a glass of lemony wine in each hand,
walking towards me always, your magnolia tree
marrying itself to the May air.

How you talked! And how I listened,
spellbound, humbled, daughterly,
to your tall tales, your wise words,
the joy of your accent, unenglish, dancey, humorous;
watching your ash hair flare and redden,
the loving litany of who we had been
making me place my hands in your warm hands,
younger than mine are now.
Then time only the moon. And the balm of dusk.
And you my mother.

A Rare Bee

I heard tell of a tale of a rare bee,
kept in a hive in a forest's soul
by a hermit – hairshirt, heart long hurt –
and that this bee made honey so pure,
when pressed to the pout of a poet
it made her profound; or if smeared
on the smile of a singer it sweetened his sound;
or when eased on the eyes of an artist,
Pablo Picasso lived and breathed;
                              so I saddled my steed.

No birds sang in the branches over my head,
though I saw the wreaths of empty nests
on the ground as I rode – girl, poet, knight –
deeper into the trees, where the white hart
was less than a ghost or a thought, was light
as the written word; legend. But what wasn't going, gone,
I mused, from the land, or the sky, or the sea?
I dismounted my bony horse to walk;
out of the silence, I fancied I heard
                              the bronze buzz of a bee.

So I came to kneel at the hermit's hive –
a little church, a tiny mosque – in a mute glade
where the loner mouthed and prayed, blind
as the sun, and saw with my own eyes
one bee dance alone on the air.
I uttered my prayer: *Give me your honey,*
bless my tongue with rhyme, poetry, song.
It flew at my mouth and stung.
Then the terrible tune of the hermit's grief.
Then a gesturing, dying bee

on the bier of a leaf.

KT-394-395

Chapter One

The fog hung around the car boot sale like
an uninvited guest. It kept most customers
away. Not that those who came found much
to spend their money on.

Josie had walked round almost all of the
stalls without finding anything she wanted
to buy. Lucky, really, because she didn't have
much money to spend.

The cold fog seeped into her bones. It was time to go home.

"Hey! You, girl – don't go home yet. You haven't looked at my stall," a voice called.

GALWAY COUNTY LIBRARIES

RUTH SYMES

Play...
If you dare

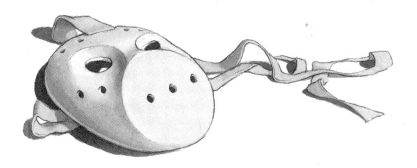

Illustrated by Stephen Player

MACDONALD YOUNG BOOKS

J117,466
£8.50

Josie looked round.

A man beckoned her. He had a straggly grey beard and wore a long black coat. A hat hid most of his face.

The man stood behind a stall Josie hadn't noticed before. She went over.

"Everyone finds what they're looking for at my stall," the man said.

He gave Josie the creeps, but his stall looked interesting. It was selling books and games.

She looked at the books first. Then she ran her fingers over the games. There were some good ones. She tried not to act too interested – in case the man upped the price.

"That's it, that's it, take your time, choose carefully," the man said.

Josie glanced up. The man grinned at her. His mouth was full of rotten, brown, jagged teeth.

She looked down. Her fingers had stopped at a hand-sized rectangular computer game. She'd wanted to buy one of these for ages but they were too expensive.

"It's probably not working," Josie told herself. No one would want to sell it if it were.

She pressed the on button. The silvery screen lit up. Black letters appeared.

So it *was* working.

The man smiled to himself and nodded his head slowly.

"You'll enjoy playing with that game," he said. "I've never had any complaints about it."

Josie pressed the off button. She didn't want to waste the batteries.

"How much?" she asked.

"Let me see," the man said. He pulled at his beard thoughtfully, "Shall we say five pounds?"

Josie quickly felt in her pocket. She brought out all the money she had. It wasn't enough.

"I've only got four pounds," she said,
"would you put the game to one side for me?
I'll run home and get the rest of the money."

The man shook his head.

Josie had to have the game.

"Please. I'll be really quick. I promise.
I live just across the park."

"Well, that game's meant for you," the
man told her. "Tell you what, I'll take what
you've got."

"Thanks," Josie said, surprised. She
handed over her money and picked up the
game. She couldn't believe she'd got
something so good for only four pounds.

The game was worth loads more than that.

She started to walk away.

"Wait!" the man called after her.

Josie stopped. She hoped he hadn't changed his mind.

"You'd better take the box it belongs in," he said. He handed her a blood-red plastic box. It had a screaming face engraved on the front.

The box was so horrible Josie didn't even want to touch it. But she had to take it.

She put the game inside the box.

"Have fun," the man said. He smiled an evil smile.

Josie turned and ran as fast as she could across the park.

When she reached the gate she looked back. She could see most of the car boot stalls, but not the one where she'd bought the game.

A thick, white fog covered the place where it had been.

Chapter Two

Josie's parents were in the kitchen making lunch when she got home.

Josie ran up the stairs and went into her room. The walls were covered with posters from her favourite film, *Aliens Save the Earth*. Models of alien spaceships hung from the ceiling. There was even a life-sized cardboard cut-out of Zargon, the alien warrior queen, standing by the window.

Josie threw her coat over a chair. Then stretched out on her bed.

She took the game out of its revolting box and dropped the box on to the floor.

She pressed the on button.

The game's silvery screen lit up and the words *"Play... If You Dare"* appeared.

Josie pressed the button again.

"Are you sure that you want to play?"

"Of course I want to," Josie muttered. Why else would she have bought the game from the creepy man?

"Press up for yes and down for no."

Josie pressed the up key pad.

"Name?"

Outside, over in the park, Josie heard a voice shouting, "Don't do it! don't do it!" Some kids must be playing.

She used the direction buttons to spell "*Jo*" for Josie.

The words *"Ready, Challenger Jo? Then let's begin"* flashed on to the screen.

GALWAY COUNTY LIBRARIES

The next moment a complicated colourful maze, with obstacles like trees, bridges and tunnels appeared.

"This looks good," Josie thought.

A tiny figure of a boy ran on to the screen. Josie watched him trying to find somewhere to hide.

J117,466

The animation for her new game was excellent. All the other games she'd seen had figures that looked more like robots than people.

But in "Play… If You Dare" the figure looked just like a real boy running. Running for his life.

Three masked men ran on to the screen.
Josie was glad that they weren't chasing her.
    In the distance she heard one of the
children in the park shouting,
"Help! Help!"

She wasn't sure how she was supposed to play the game. There weren't any instructions.

She pressed a red button and a tree fell over, blocking the path of the three chasing men. They tried to move the tree but it was too heavy. One of the hunters kicked at the tree in fury.

The boy ran off the screen. *"Well done, Challenger Jo. You have stopped the hunters – for now. Are you ready to play level 2?"*

"So the three men are hunting the boy," Josie said to herself. "And I'm supposed to help him get away."

She wanted to play level 2.

"Josie," Mum called up the stairs, "dinner's ready."

"Down in a minute," Josie shouted back. She switched off the game.

Mum came into Josie's room. She frowned at Zargon. "Nasty, ugly thing," she said.

"Zargon isn't ugly," Josie told her mum. "She's a hero."

"Hmm," Mum said, doubtfully, "she'd give me nightmares if she were in my room. Come and have your dinner."

Chapter Three

After dinner Mum and Dad went to dig over
the vegetable patch. They wanted Josie to
help too, but she said she had to do her
homework. She *did* have some homework,

but the real reason she wanted to stay
indoors was so she could play the game.
It was all she could think about.

As soon as Mum and Dad had gone
outside Josie raced upstairs and picked it up.

She pressed the on button.

"Play... If You Dare."

The children were still playing in the park. Josie heard one of them shouting, "Don't do it! They'll get you next."

"Level 2" flashed on to the screen.

This time even more obstacles appeared.

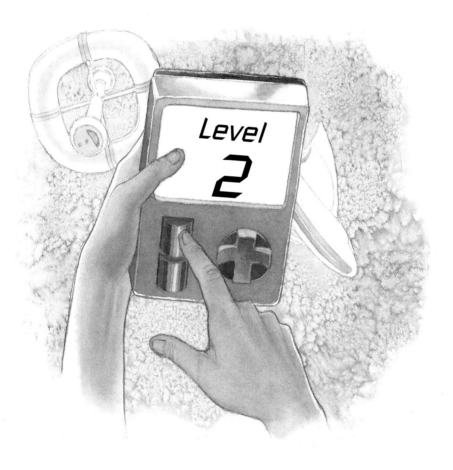

The boy soon came running. It was amazing how life-like he was. The game designer had even managed to make him look terrified.

"Help! help!" one of the children in the park shouted.

This time there were four hunters chasing the boy. Josie had seen three of them in the level 1 game but the fourth hunter was new. He wore a mask that covered his face completely.

Josie pressed the red button and toppled
a tree over to block their path. This time the
tree stopped only two of them. The other
hunters raced onwards. They were closing in
on the boy.

"The bridge, the bridge," Josie heard
a tiny voice cry.

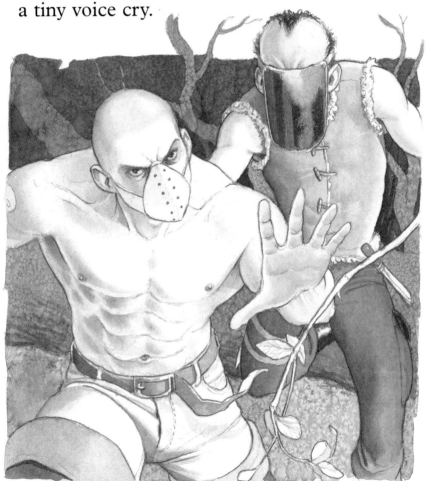

The two hunters were just running over a bridge. What would happen if...

Josie pressed the red button and the bridge collapsed. The two hunters tumbled into the rushing water below.

"That's stopped you," Josie said.

She was very pleased with her skilful playing.

Four alligators swam towards the hunters.
"Urgh!" Josie said, as she watched the
alligators start feeding. It was really gruesome.
Blood and gore crept up the screen.

Josie felt a tiny bit sick. The game designer
had been just too realistic. The children in
the park were playing a noisy game. She
could hear them screaming.

Chapter Four

"Good work, Challenger Josie."

Josie frowned. She didn't think she'd keyed in her whole name. She thought she'd only put in the first two letters.

"Level 3. Play... If You Dare."

The game was too good to stop now.

"Stop, please stop!" a tiny voice shouted and just for a moment Josie thought the voice wasn't coming from the park. It sounded like it was coming from somewhere much closer. Inside her room.

Josie pressed the play button.

Once again the boy raced on to the screen, but this time he stopped, turned to face her and cupped his hands around his mouth.

"Don't play!" he shouted in a tiny squeaky voice. "Turn the game off! Now!"

Josie almost dropped the game in surprise. Then she smiled.

How clever!

She didn't know figures in games could speak. She'd have expected it to tell her to play, not to stop playing.

The boy looked behind him then raced for the nearest bridge.

"Too late now!" he cried.

Two hunters came running on to the screen.

This time they brought a slavering, ferocious dog with them. It was straining at its chain lead. One of the hunters unclipped it.

"Do something!" the boy screamed as the dog tore towards him.

Josie pressed the red button and brought a tree down. It missed the charging dog.

The boy ran into a tunnel and the dog ran after him.

Josie could hardly bear to watch.

The dog was so close that at any moment its massive jaws would crush the boy. He would be torn to shreds. She had to do something.

Josie positioned her finger ready. As soon as the boy came out of the tunnel she pressed the red button.

The tunnel caved in.

"Yes!" Josie shouted.

It had been a close thing. But she'd managed to save the boy. Without her skilful playing he'd have been dog food.

Chapter Five

"Congratulations, Challenger Josie. Now it's your turn to play the real game."

'The real game?' Josie thought. Hadn't she been playing the real game?

"Turn it off!" the boy's voice cried. "Quick, before it traps you inside it like it trapped me!"

"Huh?" Josie said.

She pressed the off button, but nothing happened. She pressed it again. She started to feel scared. Very scared. She turned the game over and flicked open the back flap.

No batteries!

"Your turn now, Challenger Josie."

"Put it in the box!" the boy shouted.

Josie tried to put the game back into its red box. But the lid wouldn't open.

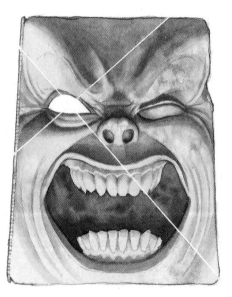

The screaming face on the box started to smile. No, not smile – leer. As one eye slowly winked at her.

Josie screamed.

"Time to change places, Challenger Josie," the screen read.

Josie's hands were starting to fade. She could feel herself draining away.

"No!" she cried.

She had to do something – fast! She looked at Zargon. The alien queen would know what to do... And suddenly Josie knew!

"Take Zargon instead. She's a much better player than me," she told the game screen.

"Zargon?"

Feeling as heavy as lead, Josie dragged herself off the bed and positioned the game so it could see Zargon. She didn't go too close, in case it saw that Zargon was only a cardboard cut-out.

"Zargon will be a worthy game player. Come, Challenger Zargon.
Play... If You Dare."

Zargon disappeared.

The hunted boy was ejected from the game and fell, life-sized – THUD! – into Josie's room.

He scuttled into a corner and stared in terror at the game.

Josie couldn't move. She felt sick with fear. Her heart thumped loudly as she waited for the game to realize it had been tricked.

It happened almost immediately. Smoke began to fume out of the game. It made strange hissing sounds.

GALWAY COUNTY LIBRARIES

"Error! Error!" the screen read.

"Player not human!
Shut down! Shut down!
Shu..."

The game melted in on itself until there was nothing left but a crumpled ball. Then, with a last hiss, it disappeared. The red plastic box dissolved into blood-red gloop and then was gone too.

Josie stared at the place where it had been.

"It's over!" the boy whispered. "The game's finally over and you..." he looked up at Josie. "You won."

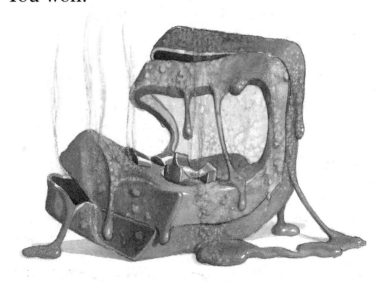